POTENTIAL ENERGY VS. KINETIC ENERGY PHYSICS MADE SIMPLE

4th Grade
Children's Physics Books

BABY PROFESSOR
EDUCATION KIDS

Speedy Publishing LLC

40 E. Main St. #1156

Newark, DE 19711

www.speedypublishing.com

Copyright 2017

In this book, we're going to talk about the difference between potential energy versus kinetic energy. So, let's get right to it!

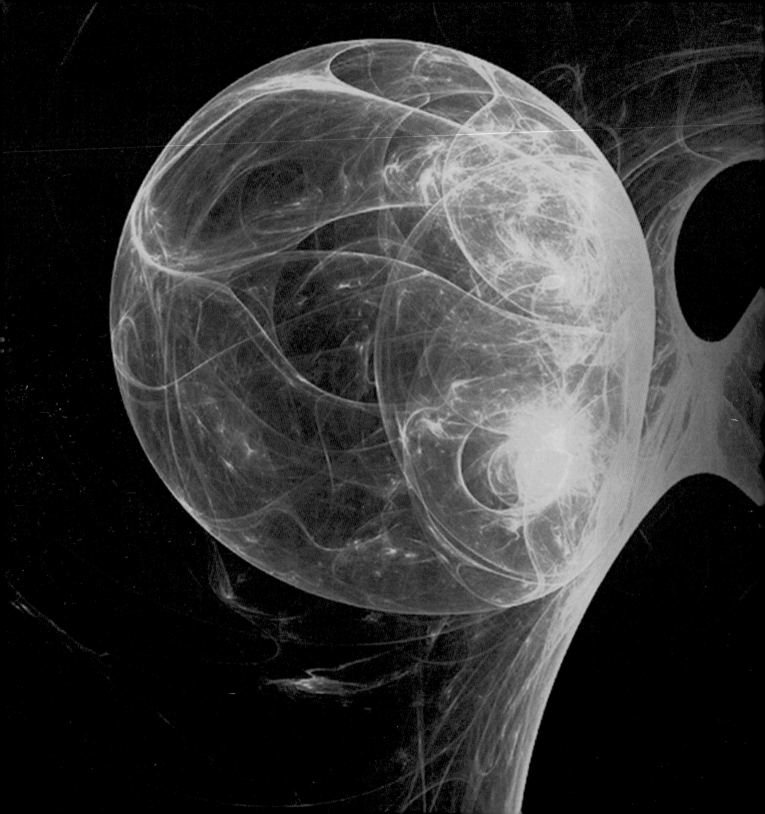

The difference between potential energy and kinetic energy is basically the difference between not moving and moving. When an object isn't moving, it has energy stored in it that can be released under the right conditions. This energy is called potential energy. When an object starts to move, its potential energy starts converting to kinetic energy.

The law of conservation of energy states that energy can't be formed nor can it be destroyed. So, as potential energy is converted to kinetic energy, the energy isn't created. It's not destroyed either. Instead, it is transformed from one type of energy to another.

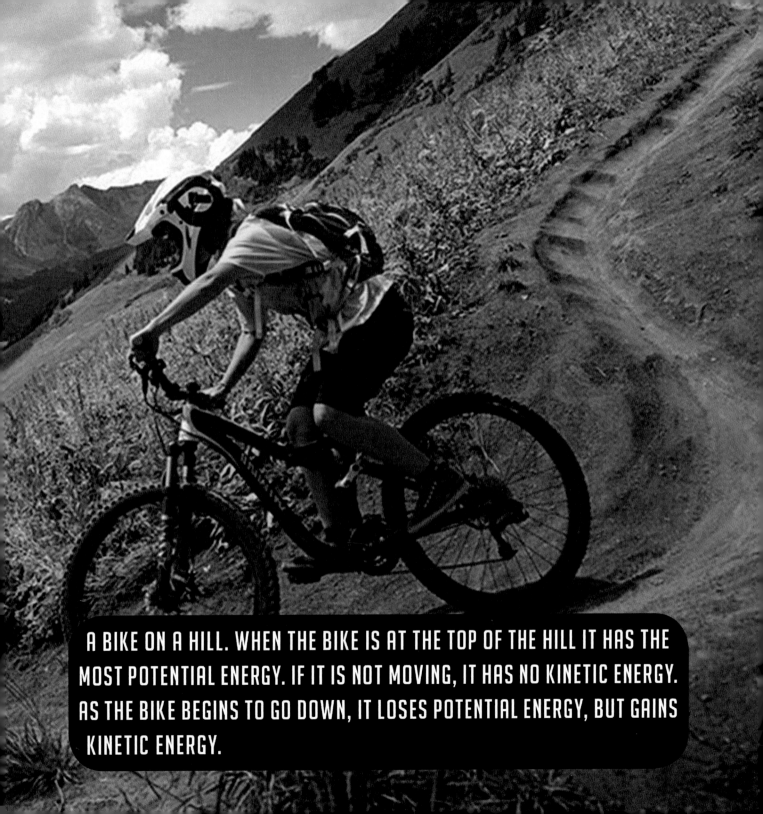

A BIKE ON A HILL. WHEN THE BIKE IS AT THE TOP OF THE HILL IT HAS THE MOST POTENTIAL ENERGY. IF IT IS NOT MOVING, IT HAS NO KINETIC ENERGY. AS THE BIKE BEGINS TO GO DOWN, IT LOSES POTENTIAL ENERGY, BUT GAINS KINETIC ENERGY.

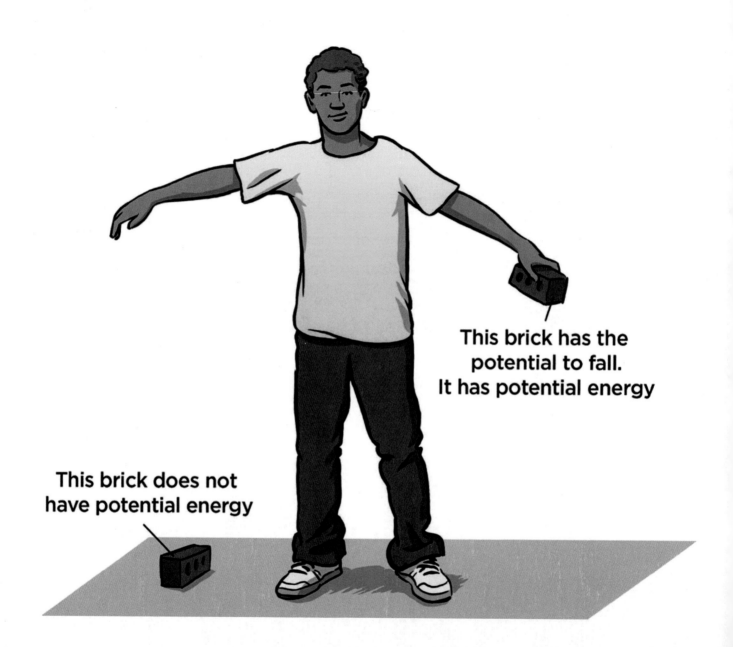

WHAT IS POTENTIAL ENERGY?

An object has energy stored in it that is due to either its position or its state. That stored energy is called potential energy. A car at the top of a ramp, a basketball held above your head, and a rubber band that is stretched but hasn't been let go of yet are all examples of potential energy due to position. A chemical that hasn't reacted with another chemical yet, has potential energy due to its state.

HOW IS POTENTIAL ENERGY MEASURED?

The joule, which is written as "J" is the unit of measurement that's used when describing potential energy.

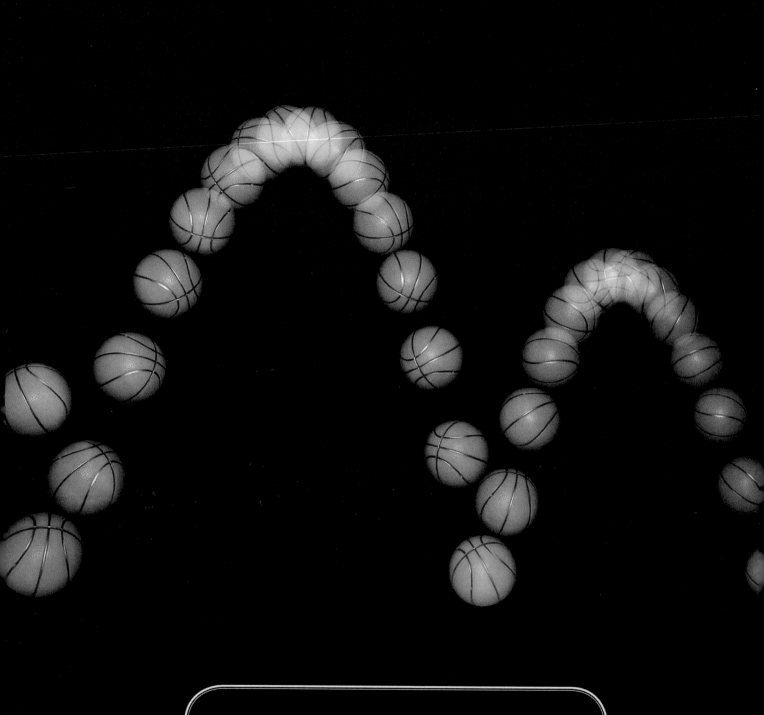

A BOUNCING BALL

HOW IS POTENTIAL ENERGY DIFFERENT FROM KINETIC ENERGY?

When an object is in motion, it has energy and that energy is described as kinetic energy. Potential energy is the energy the object has stored that is not yet in motion. Potential energy begins to convert to kinetic energy as soon as an object starts to move. So, in summary, objects that are not moving have potential energy. Objects that are moving have kinetic energy.

A WAGON ON A HILL

Suppose you have a toy wagon and your driveway is on a hill. When the wagon is positioned at the highest point on the driveway, it has the highest amount of potential energy. If the wagon isn't moving, it doesn't have any kinetic energy yet.

WAGON ON A HILL

INFLUENZA OUTBREAK 1900S

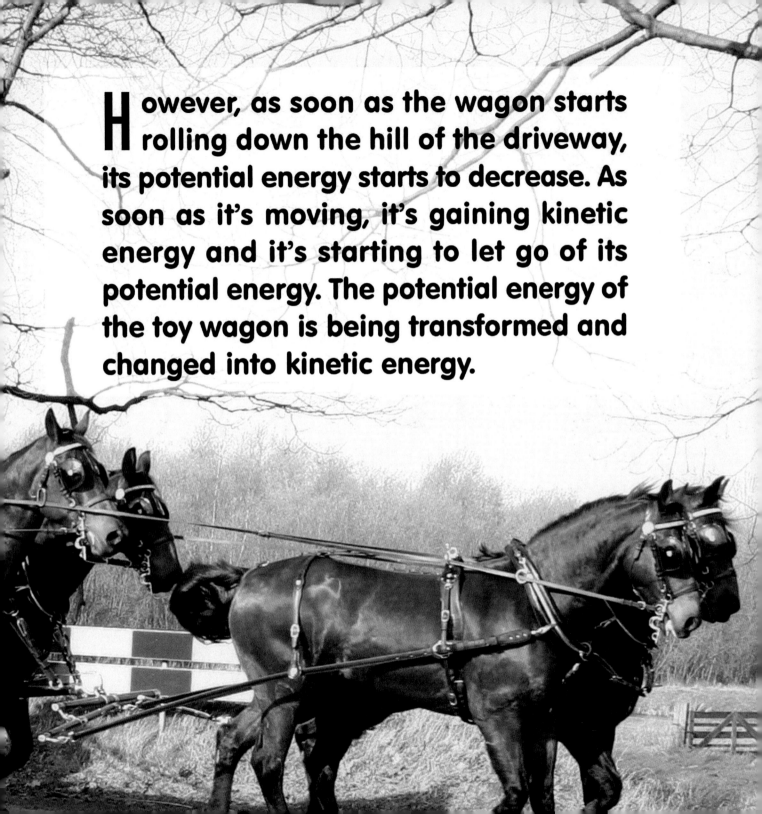

However, as soon as the wagon starts rolling down the hill of the driveway, its potential energy starts to decrease. As soon as it's moving, it's gaining kinetic energy and it's starting to let go of its potential energy. The potential energy of the toy wagon is being transformed and changed into kinetic energy.

WHAT IS GRAVITATIONAL POTENTIAL ENERGY?

The mass of an object, its height from the ground, and the Earth's gravity are all related to a type of potential energy that is referred to as gravitational potential energy or GPE. To find out the GPE of an object we can use this equation:

- GPE = mass of an object times its gravity times the height from which it would be dropped

POTENTIAL ENERGY

POTENTIAL ENERGY TRANSFORMING TO KINETIC ENERGY

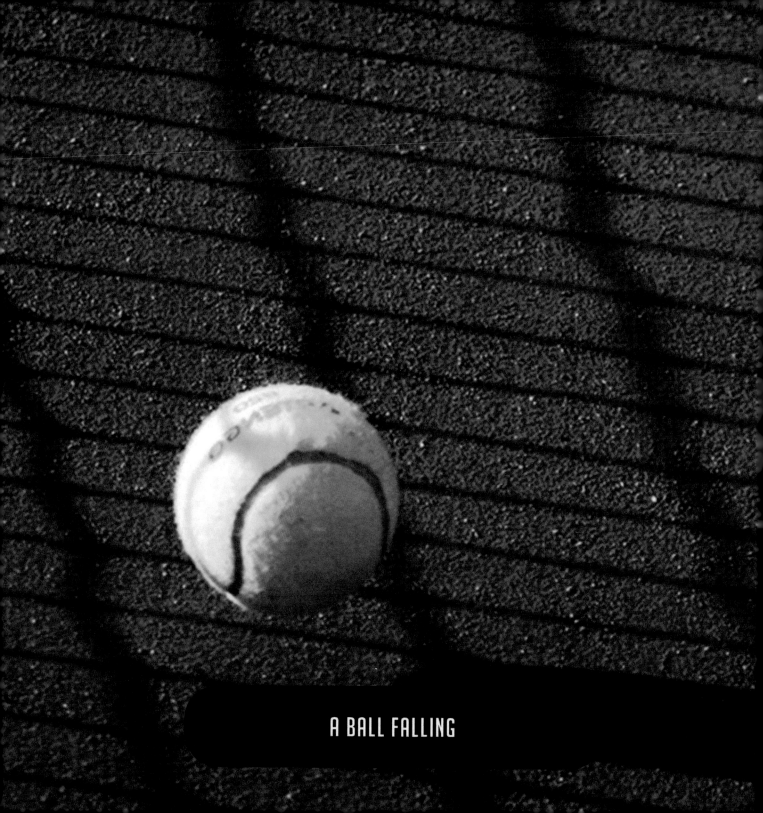

A BALL FALLING

In this formula, the variable "g" is measured as gravity's standard acceleration on Earth, which is equivalent to 9.8 meters per second squared written in symbols as 9.8 m/s2. The height is simply the measurement of how far the object could fall if it did fall. It could be the distance from the object to the ground or the distance from a surface where an object is positioned to the ground.

Notice that the mass of the object needs to be expressed in kilograms and the distance it can fall should be expressed in meters.

Here are two sample problems.

- What is the GPE of a rock that has a mass of 4 kilograms if it's sitting on top of a 40-meter-high hill?

    GPE = m • g • h

    GPE = 4 kg • 9.8 m/s2 • 40 m

    GPE = 1,568 J

WEIGHT IN KILOGRAMS

TABLETS

O **What is the GPE of a piano that has a mass of 220 kilograms and is held by a crane 60 meters in the air?**

GPE = m • g • h
GPE = 220 kg • 9.8 m/s2 • 60 m
GPE = 129,360 J

THE RELATIONSHIP BETWEEN POTENTIAL ENERGY AND WORK

L et's say you lift a potted plant up from the ground and put it on a table. Since the potted plant was displaced it took work to get it up on the table. The potential energy of the potted plant once you get it up on the table will be equivalent to the measurement of the work it took for you to get it there.

Gravitational Potential Energy and Work

$f_{a(ext)}$

$f_g = mg$

Δy

Work = Change in U_g

$fd \cos 0 = mg\Delta y$

$mg\Delta y$

CHEMICAL ENERGY

OTHER TYPES OF POTENTIAL ENERGY

CHEMICAL

The energy that is stored within the molecular bonds of chemicals is called chemical potential energy. It's stored there until the chemical reacts with another chemical and the energy is emitted.

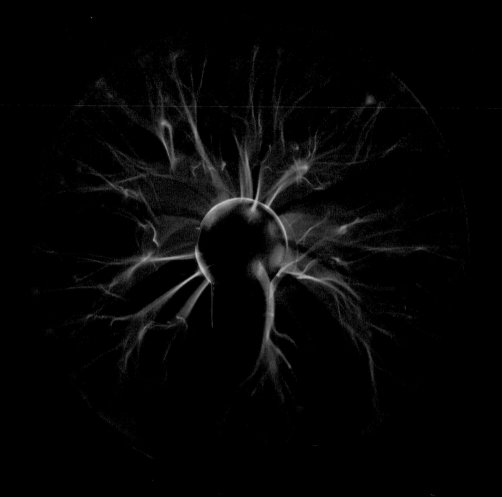

NUCLEAR

The energy stored in the electrons and protons of an atom is called nuclear potential energy.

ELECTRIC

Objects can have an electrical charge. That charge is the object's potential energy or its capacity for work.

ELASTIC

When materials are either stretched or compressed, they have elastic potential energy. Rubber bands and different types of springs all have elastic potential energy. The formula for Elastic Potential Energy is PE = ½ • k • x2 where k represents the spring constant and x represents its amount of compression.

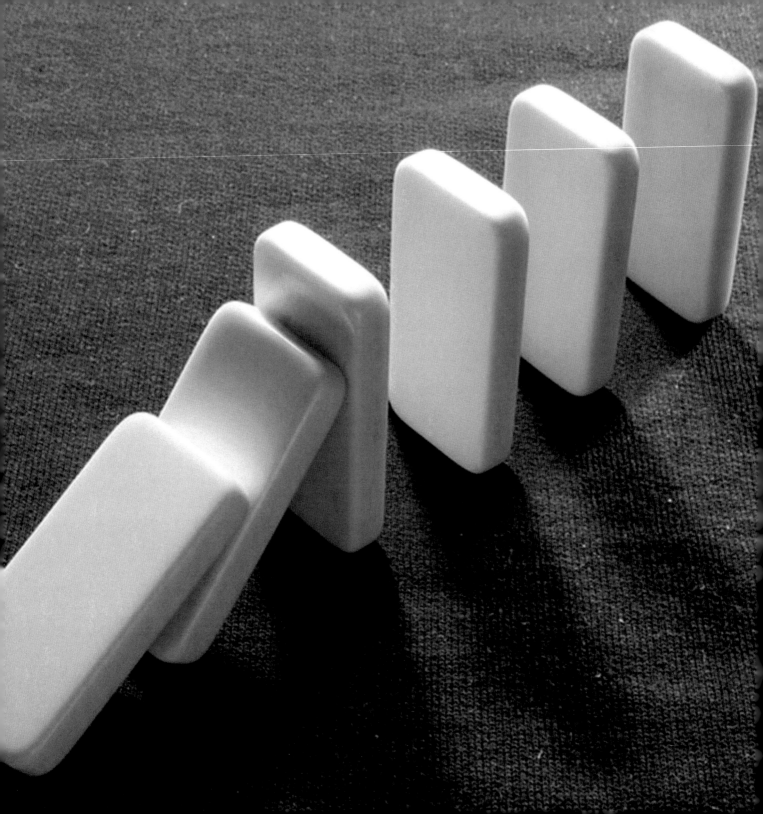

WHAT IS KINETIC ENERGY?

As soon as an object starts moving, its potential energy begins to transform to kinetic energy. If it continues to move at a consistent velocity, it will keep a constant kinetic energy.

To calculate an object's kinetic energy, you would need to have the object's mass as well as the velocity that the object is traveling. Since the velocity is squared in the formula it has a huge impact on the final measurement of kinetic energy.

ICE SKATING

HOW IS KINETIC ENERGY MEASURED?

Just as with potential energy, kinetic energy is measured using the joule, abbreviated as *J*. It's the standard unit of measurement for both work and energy. Kinetic energy is not a vector, which simply means it doesn't have a direction. It just has magnitude or quantity.

HOW IS KINETIC ENERGY DIFFERENT FROM POTENTIAL ENERGY?

The main difference is that in order to have kinetic energy an object must be moving. That's why velocity is a critical component of the formula for kinetic energy. Velocity is not related to potential energy. As an object with potential energy begins to move, its potential energy is converted into kinetic energy.

SLEDDING DOWN A HILL

Imagine that you're in a sled on a snowy hill. You're at the very top about to go down. At this point the sled you're sitting in is at the peak of its potential energy. Now the sled starts to slide down the hill. As it does, its kinetic energy is increasing and its potential energy is decreasing. By the time it gets to the bottom, it has the most kinetic energy. As its kinetic energy increased, its potential energy decreased.

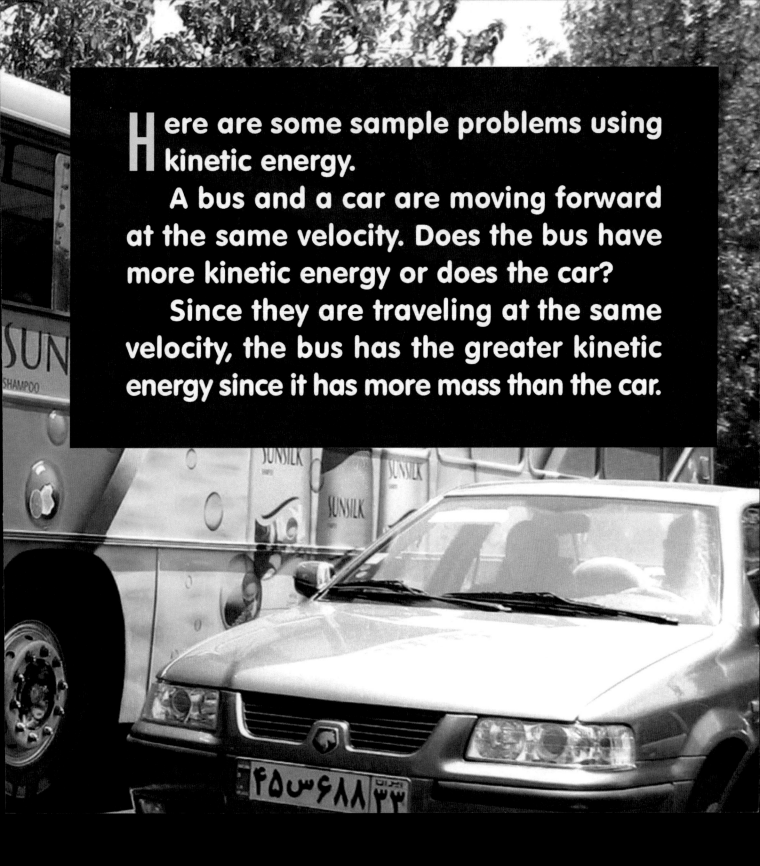

H ere are some sample problems using kinetic energy.

A bus and a car are moving forward at the same velocity. Does the bus have more kinetic energy or does the car?

Since they are traveling at the same velocity, the bus has the greater kinetic energy since it has more mass than the car.

A stone has a mass of 5 kilograms and is moving at a rate of 8 m/s. What is the stone's kinetic energy?

$$KE = \frac{1}{2} \cdot m \cdot v^2$$
$$KE = \frac{1}{2} \cdot 5 \text{ kg} \cdot (8 \text{ m/s})^2$$
$$KE = 160 \text{ J}$$

A girl has a mass of 40 kilograms and she's running at 2 m/s. What is her kinetic energy?

$$KE = \frac{1}{2} \cdot m \cdot v2$$
$$KE = \frac{1}{2} \cdot 40 \text{ kg} \cdot (2 \text{ m/s})2$$
$$KE = 80 \text{ J}$$

ARISTOTLE

FASCINATING FACTS ABOUT POTENTIAL AND KINETIC ENERGY

○ The term "potential energy" was first used in the 19th century by William Rankine, a Scottish scientist.

○ Aristotle, the philosopher from Ancient Greek civilization theorized about potential energy.

- If an object's mass is doubled, its kinetic energy is also doubled.

- If an object's speed is doubled, its kinetic energy is four times as great.

- The word "**kinesis**" comes from the Greek language and means motion and this is why the phrase "kinetic energy" means the energy of motion.

ENERGY OF MOTION

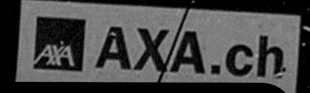

CAR COLLISION

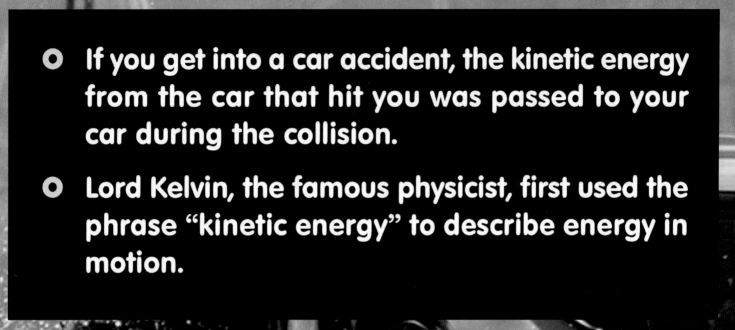

- If you get into a car accident, the kinetic energy from the car that hit you was passed to your car during the collision.

- Lord Kelvin, the famous physicist, first used the phrase "kinetic energy" to describe energy in motion.

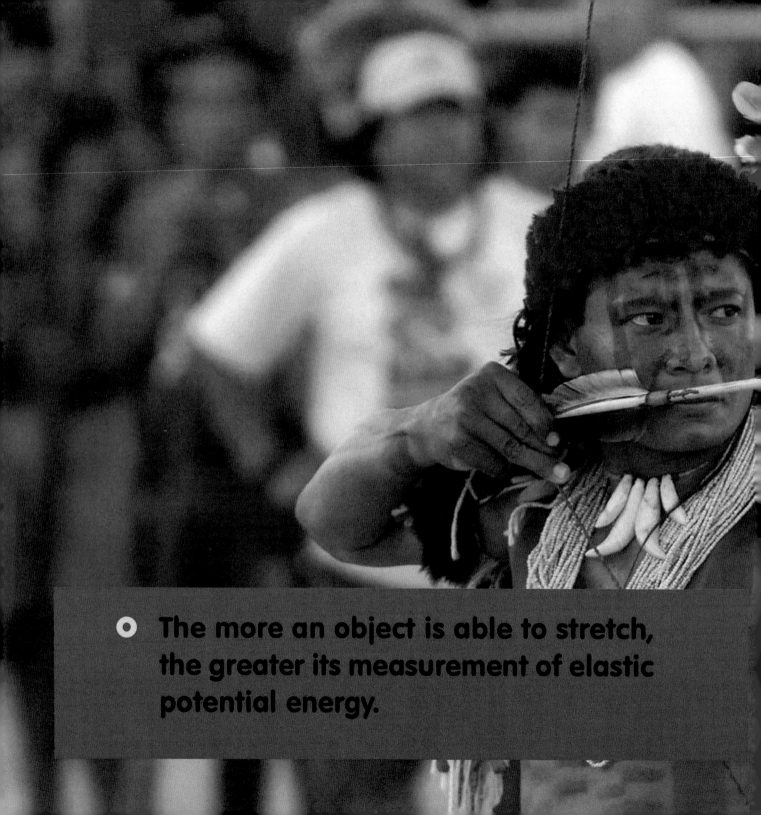

● **The more an object is able to stretch, the greater its measurement of elastic potential energy.**

When an archer uses a bow and arrow, the potential energy from his or her hand transfers to the bow, when it's grabbed and pulled backwards.

- A trampoline and a bungee cord are both examples of elastic potential energy.

- Kinetic energy can be described as either translational or rotational. Translational kinetic energy is motion that takes place through space. Motion that is centered on an axis is called rotational kinetic energy.

Awesome! Now you know more about potential energy and kinetic energy. You can find more Physics books from Baby Professor by searching the website of your favorite book retailer.

Visit

BABY PROFESSOR
EDUCATION KIDS

www.BabyProfessorBooks.com

to download Free Baby Professor eBooks and view
our catalog of new and exciting Children's Books